Put Beginning Readers on the Right Track with
ALL ABOARD READING™

The All Aboard Reading series is especially designed for beginning readers. Written by noted authors and illustrated in full color, these are books that children really want to read—books to excite their imagination, expand their interests, make them laugh, and support their feelings. With fiction and nonfiction stories that are high interest and curriculum-related, All Aboard Reading books offer something for every young reader. And with four different reading levels, the All Aboard Reading series lets you choose which books are most appropriate for your children and their growing abilities.

Picture Readers
Picture Readers have super-simple texts, with many nouns appearing as rebus pictures. At the end of each book are 24 flash cards—on one side is a rebus picture; on the other side is the written-out word.

Station Stop 1
Station Stop 1 books are best for children who have just begun to read. Simple words and big type make these early reading experiences more comfortable. Picture clues help children to figure out the words on the page. Lots of repetition throughout the text helps children to predict the next word or phrase—an essential step in developing word recognition.

Station Stop 2
Station Stop 2 books are written specifically for children who are reading with help. Short sentences make it easier for early readers to understand what they are reading. Simple plots and simple dialogue help children with reading comprehension.

Station Stop 3
Station Stop 3 books are perfect for children who are reading alone. With longer text and harder words, these books appeal to children who have mastered basic reading skills. More complex stories captivate children who are ready for more challenging books.

In addition to All Aboard Reading books, look for All Aboard Math Readers™ (fiction stories that teach math concepts children are learning in school) and All Aboard Science Readers™ (nonfiction books that explore the most fascinating science topics in age-appropriate language).

All Aboard for happy reading!

Photo credits: p. 3 AFP/Corbis; p. 5 Dan Loh/AP Wide World Photo; p. 11 John Storey/TimePix; p. 15 Bettmann/Corbis; p. 18 Robert Beck/Sports Illustrated; p. 21 Pearson Learning; p. 25 Ezra Shaw/Allsport Photography / Getty Images; p. 28 David Young-Wolf/PhotoEdit; p. 31 Robert Beck/Sports Illustrated; p. 33 Ezra Shaw/Allsport Photography / Getty Images; p. 35 AFP/Corbis; p. 38 Roger L. Wollenberg/UPI United Press International; p. 41 Sebastian Artz / Getty Images; p. 42 Paul Bearce/AP Wide World Photo; p. 43 Courtesy of Clinton Presidential Materials Project; p. 45 AFP/Corbis; p. 47 Pearson Learning

Library of Congress Cataloging-in-Publication Data is available.

ISBN 0-448-43160-2 (pbk)   A B C D E F G H I J
ISBN 0-448-43231-5 (GB)   A B C D E F G H I J

All Aboard Reading™
Station Stop 3

TONY HAWK
RIDE ANDY MACDONALD
TO THE TOP

By Alice Dieterich

Grosset & Dunlap • New York

Chapter 1: Twice as Tricky

What's better than watching a pro skater flip through the air like some kind of crazed superhero? How about watching two pros tear through their tricks together?

That's what fans at the 1999 X Games came to see. All eyes were on Tony Hawk and Andy Macdonald, two skateboarders who slammed their way to fame with their show-stopping moves. Now they were teaming up for the third time in the X Games to compete in the Vert Doubles Competition.

Each team gets two runs on the half-pipe—two chances to impress the judges. They must have thought they were seeing double when Tony and Andy began their first run. The pair whipped up and down

Andy and Tony flying high at the X Games

the ramp, landing several mirrored tricks by doing the same stunt at the same time.

Then Tony and Andy pulled off an impressive board transfer. Tony held up his board. Andy flew in, grabbing Tony's board and putting it under his own feet with one hand. At the same time, Andy held onto his own board with his other hand. The crowd loved it.

But the contest wasn't over yet. The other teams had great runs, too. Tony and Andy would have to pull out all the stops if they were going to bag the gold.

Tony and Andy had been practicing some new tricks for their second run. In practice, they usually wiped out. Would they be able to get it together for the games?

They did—in a big way. Tony spun a huge 720—two complete spins in the air—while soaring over Andy. While Tony flew overhead, Andy spun an Indy-360 underneath.

Then came the highlight of the run. Tony came grinding across the top of the ramp. Andy held out his board. Tony jumped on Andy's board and finished the grind. The crowd went crazy.

The judges liked what they saw, too. They gave Tony and Andy a score of 93.50 out of 100 for their second run. They had earned their third gold medal in the Vert Doubles competition!

A reporter for ESPN once said, "Individually, Tony Hawk and Andy Macdonald are giants in the sport of skateboarding; together, they are unstoppable."

So how exactly did two American boys become unstoppable skateboarding giants? The road to success was paved with practice and hard work—and a whole lot of fun.

Vert Doubles

In this competition, skateboarders pick partners and create routines on the vertical halfpipe—a u-shaped ramp with steep sides. If the team's timing is off even by a little, the skateboarders can collide, risking injury and ruining their run. That's why, in the X Games, teamwork is an important part of the final score.

Chapter 2: Birth of the Birdman

In 1982, the skateboard world buzzed with the news that a fourteen-year-old skater named Tony Hawk had turned pro. What was so special about this kid from California? Tony Hawk showed the world—and skateboarding would never be the same.

Even though he turned pro before he finished high school, for a while Tony was an ordinary kid. He was born on May 12, 1968, in Carlsbad, California. His father, Frank, was a salesman and his mom, Nancy, taught at a community college. He grew up with his sisters, Lenore and Pat, and his brother, Steve.

Tony was the youngest kid in the family, and also the most challenging. He was a tall, skinny boy with a lot of energy. He was easily distracted and got into a lot of trouble in school.

The school figured out Tony's problem when he was about eight years old. Tony was a gifted kid, and his regular classes bored him. Tony started taking harder classes to challenge his mind. Now he needed to find something to challenge his body, too.

Tony's parents hoped that playing sports would help him use up his extra energy. They encouraged him to try baseball and basketball. But he became bored while he sat on the bench or ran drills at practice. He wasn't good at playing by the rules of organized sports.

Then his brother, Steve, did something that would change Tony's life. Steve gave Tony a skateboard. Tony hopped on the blue fiberglass banana board and took

Tony and his father, Frank

off. From that moment on, he spent every
chance he could get skateboarding with
friends at skateparks, on the streets, and
even in drained swimming pools.

Tony worried he would let his dad
down when he dropped out of Little
League. But Frank Hawk supported
his son. He drove Tony to skateboard

contests. He built ramps for Tony to perform tricks on. He even started two skateboarding organizations and set up competitions.

With his family's support, Tony's career soared. Of course, it took a lot of practice, too. Tony tried to master the tricks of other skateboarders. As he improved, he even made up tricks of his own.

But the road to the pros wasn't always smooth. Other skateboarders gave Tony a hard time for doing his own thing. He was also teased for being a very skinny kid. He had to wear elbow pads on his knees, because regular kneepads were too big for his legs. After a while, though, stuff like skinny knees didn't matter. Tony became such a skilled rider that he earned the respect of other skateboarders. They even started imitating his tricks!

While Tony was working on becoming a better skateboarder, the popularity of skateboarding was increasing. Early on, big toy companies were the main makers of skateboards and equipment. But in the 1970s, smaller companies began springing up. They made cool boards, clothes, and other gear. And they found that the best way to sell their boards was to get the best riders to use them in competition.

So the skateboard companies began to sponsor riders. They paid riders to use their products. This was good for the company and good for the skateboarders, too. A skater with a big sponsor could earn enough money to quit work and skate full time. Usually, a skater with a big sponsorship was considered a "pro."

That's just what happened to Tony. By the time he was fourteen, he was placing first or second in every competition he entered. This got the attention of Powell Peralta, a leading skateboard company. They sponsored Tony, and he went pro. He was nicknamed "Birdman" because of his last name, Hawk, and because when he skated, it looked like he was flying.

After he turned pro, Tony's career went soaring, too. He bought a house when he was a senior in high school. A few years later, he got married and had a son, Riley. Tony was on top of the world. But like every skater knows, what goes up has to hit the ground sometime, and Tony soon found himself facing some tough times.

From Surfboards to Skateboards

Skateboarding as we know it began in 1958 with surfers in Southern California. When they water was too calm to ride the waves, surfers figured out a way to surf on land. They took small planks of wood, attached wheels to each end, and hit the boardwalks. Toy manufacturers caught on to the trend and started developing "sidewalk surfboards." Over time, the boards became known simply as "skateboards."

Some of the first skateboarders

Chapter 3: A Snowy Struggle

Tony Hawk may have found money and fame at an early age. But for Andy Macdonald, those things didn't come so quickly.

Andy was born on July 31, 1973, in Boston, Massachusetts. The son of divorced parents, Andy spent summers with his father in Michigan and the rest of the time with his mother in Boston. If it wasn't for Andy's mom, he might not be rocketing across halfpipes today.

"My mom made the insane mistake of buying me a skateboard when I was twelve, and it's all been downhill from there," Andy joked in an interview.

Andy flipped for his new board, but he was also a pretty well-rounded athlete in high school. He tried swimming, soccer, wrestling, and gymnastics. Andy learned discipline, coordination, and sportsmanship through these sports—but skating was always his favorite.

During his junior year, Andy decided to devote most of his time to skateboarding. By the time he was seventeen, he had entered several competitions. Andy found he could keep pace with the big boys and dreamed of going pro.

Andy's mom didn't think he could earn enough money skateboarding to make a living at it. One thing was certain: Andy couldn't become a pro if he stayed in New England. The cold, wet weather in Massachusetts made for slippery skateboarding. Andy built his own skateboard ramps out of snow and wood in the winter, but they just didn't cut it. Andy needed to go to sunny California, where most of the pros skated. So he drove out west right after high school, in 1992.

Andy had no sponsorship, no job, and not much money in his pockets. He landed in San Diego and began looking for a job—any job. He found one at Sea World, wearing the Shamu the Whale costume! The outfit was sweaty, and the

Andy soars through the air

pay wasn't great, but it was enough to get by. In his free time, Andy skated with the pro boarders who lived in the area. He also hooked up with a group of pool skaters—boarders who trick in drained swimming pools.

Andy quickly learned more and more tricks. He skated in lots of different places, and he entered more competitions. But no matter how hard he tried, or how fast he flew, there was one obstacle Andy couldn't conquer. Nobody wanted to sponsor him.

Finally, in 1994, a man named Mike McGill noticed Andy. Mike owned a sports company, and he wanted Andy to start a line of skateboard products with him. Andy agreed, and he and Mike launched Human Skateboards with Andy's pro line.

Andy's dream of becoming a pro skater had come true, but his really big break was still to come.

The Ollie

The Ollie, created by Alan "Ollie" Gelfand, is the most basic skateboard trick. When performing an Ollie, a rider taps the tail of the board on the ground with his back foot, which forces the board into the air. The board is balanced with the front foot. The board looks like it's stuck to the rider's feet as he flies through the air. Most skateboard tricks have evolved from this basic technique.

A skateboarder performing an Ollie

Chapter 4: Highs and Lows

In the early 1990s, Andy Macdonald was starting his climb to skateboarding superstardom. Around the same time, Tony Hawk found his fame slipping.

In 1990, Tony had a hot career as a vert skater. But in 1991, the popularity of vert skating took a nosedive. Skateboarding parks with vert ramps had become too expensive to keep open, and many closed down. Because skaters had no parks in which to skate, they took to the street. In the early '90s, street skating became the rage. It seemed as though nobody cared about vert skating anymore.

Because Tony was known as a vert skater, he wasn't getting paid to skate as much as he used to. He and his family were barely getting by. But Tony didn't give up. In 1992, he started his own skateboard-manufacturing company. Birdhouse—a home for the Birdman—sold skateboards and other skateboarding equipment. It took a while for things to get off the ground, but as street skating became more popular, Tony's business grew. By 1995, Birdhouse had become a successful company.

That same year, vert skating bounced back, partly because the X Games aired on TV for the first time. Now more people than ever could see vert skaters perform—and they couldn't believe their eyes. The high-flying tricks and spins in the vert competitions were absolutely amazing.

That's when Tony came hurtling back onto the scene. In the first X Games, he won the gold medal in the vert competition. He also placed second in the street competition. That silenced any critics who thought that the Birdman could only spin and fly through the air vert-style. Tony Hawk was back in a big way.

Tony kept skating in competitions and winning medals. Birdhouse became one of the biggest skateboard companies in the world. By 1999, Tony was flying high— and this time he was determined to stay on top.

Tony's career as a pro skater soared at the X Games on June 27, 1999, when he competed in the best trick competition. The contest is a forty-five-minute "jam." Skaters use the time to impress the judges by performing any tricks they want.

Tony started his run with a heart-stopping 720—two spins in midair. There

Tony on the half pipe

was only one place left to go. Tony decided
to try the sickest trick any skater had ever
tried—the 900. To do it, he'd have to
launch his body off the ramp, spin two and
a half times in the air, and land back on
the ramp. No one had ever done it before
without wiping out—not even Tony. But
he was determined to pull it off.

"900! 900!" the crowd chanted. Skateboarders banged their boards on the vert

ramp. Tony flew down the ramp, spun once, twice . . . and then bailed. He tried again. He rocketed down the halfpipe, executed two and a half spins . . . and crashed. He tried and tried, but he couldn't get it. Before he knew it, his forty-five minutes were up.

But the crowd and the skaters wanted Tony to have another chance. They began to boo. The announcer, caught up in the excitement, yelled, "This is the X Games. We make up the rules as we go along. Let's give him another try!"

Tony tried again . . . and his board slid out from under him. The same thing happened again. But he refused to give up.

On the eleventh try, Tony cruised down the ramp and came up the other side. He repeated the maneuver twice to build up power and speed. Then he launched himself into the air. He spun two and a half times . . . and almost lurched off his board as he landed.

But the Birdman caught his balance. He glided safely to the other side of the ramp. He had conquered the 900! The crowd went crazy, and the other skateboarders rushed the ramp to congratulate him. Surrounded by his friends and family, Tony said, "This is the best day of my life!"

Street skating

Street Skateboarding vs. Vert Skateboarding

Street skateboarding is exactly what it sounds like. Street skaters ride on streets, curbs, and handrails. In competitions, they usually perform their tricks on a course that is designed to look like a street. They are judged on the difficulty of the tricks and on the style. Vert skating takes place on ramps or halfpipes— u-shaped ramps that are at least eight feet tall and rounded in the middle. Skaters perform maneuvers in the air at the top of the vert ramp, land back on the ramp, and ride to the other side to perform another trick.

Chapter 5: Friends and Rivals

In 1999, Tony Hawk shocked everyone at the X Games. A few years earlier, in 1996, Andy Macdonald had done the same thing.

Andy had turned pro in 1994, but he wasn't a superstar yet. He competed in the first X Games in 1995. But he lost the gold medal in the vert competition to Tony that year. Nobody really expected Andy to beat the legendary Birdman, anyway.

But Andy came back strong the next year. He faced Tony in the vert competition and stole the gold. Fame finally came calling, and Andy was ready.

"That's when people started to notice me," Andy said. He left Human skateboards and signed deals with several different companies. Soon Andy was promoting boards, shoes, helmets, and clothes. Now he had enough money—and confidence—to keep living his dream.

Tony and Andy were friends before competing against each other in the X Games. They have remained friends,

Andy's balancing act

but when Andy beat Tony in 1996, a rivalry began. Tony took back the gold in the vert competition in 1997. The next year, Andy won it. People tuned in to the X Games to watch Tony and Andy face off. But the competition never got ugly.

"As long as he wins, or I win, it's all good," Andy told ESPN.

In 1997, fans of Tony and Andy had another reason to tune in to the games. That's when the vert doubles competition began. While Tony and Andy liked to challenge each other in the verts, they couldn't resist teaming up together. They took the gold in 1997 and captured it every year for the next five years. No other skating team could beat the dynamic duo of Hawk and Macdonald.

The two skateboarders have a lot of respect for each other. Andy has said that

Best pals Andy and Tony

they work well together because their styles are so different. He praises Tony's high-flying spins, while Tony is a fan of Andy's "gnarly combos."

If you want proof of their friendship, just tune in to the X Games. Tony retired from competition in 1999, but he continues to skate the Vert Doubles with Andy. Looks like friends who skate together stay together!

The X Games

The X Games were created by the sports network ESPN in 1995 because extreme sports were becoming more popular. Extreme sports include BMX bike riding, motorcross, snowboarding, in-line skating, street luge, and skateboarding. At the X Games, athletes compete for medals and hope to become the best in their extreme sports. But along with the glory comes risk, as athletes try to keep from wiping out as they perform dangerous stunts.

Flying high at the X Games

Chapter 6: Andy's World Record

Some of Andy's greatest moments happened at the X Games with Tony Hawk. But in 1999, Andy made skateboarding history on his own.

Andy had a dream. He wanted to hold a Guinness World Record for the longest jump on a skateboard. No one had tried it before. Andy would be the first. At a friend's home in Michigan in October, Andy jumped 52 feet 10 inches and soared over four parked cars. Andy had set a world record!

The stunt was called "the first Evel-Knievel-like skateboard stunt ever performed." Dangling a record like that in front of other skateboarders was like dangling a bone in front of a dog. The world's best skateboarders challenged

Andy. On March 27, 2000, in Lake Havasu, Arizona, twenty of them tried to beat Andy's record. They took practice jumps using new and specially designed equipment to help them jump longer and higher. Andy was there, too. He and some of the other riders felt so comfortable with the practice jump that they even tried a few tricks while flying through the air.

The riders were jumping far, but not as far as 52 feet 10 inches. They raised the height of the ramp and pushed it out farther. Only three skaters—including Andy—successfully landed the jump. They had all matched Andy's record. But could anyone beat it?

Each rider got seven chances to set a new record. No one could beat it—except Andy. He hurtled through the air like a human cannonball and landed at 56 feet 10¾ inches. He had beaten his own record!

In January 2001, a skater named Brian Patch broke Andy's record. But Andy was still the first athlete with the guts to do it. He had gone where no skateboarder had gone before—and set the standard for the future.

Andy shows off his moves

Chapter 7: Video Games and PSAs

What's so great about being a pro skateboarder? It's a life full of gnarly wipeouts, broken bones, hard work, and empty pockets. But if you're lucky enough to make it big, you might get to star in your own video game—or even meet the President.

Tony Hawk's life has had as many ups and downs as a skater on a halfpipe. He and his wife, Cindy, split up in 1994. Tony's dad, Frank, died in 1995. Tony almost lost his career when vert skating tanked in the early '90s.

These days, Tony's life is at an all-time high. He doesn't compete much any more, but he's still the king of the skateboarding world. He started the Tony Hawk Foundation to help create public skateboarding parks for kids. His goal is to provide kids with safe places to practice.

Tony has also taken his act to the road, first with Tony Hawk's Gigantic Skatepark Tour. In 2002 he launched the insane Boom Boom HuckJam tour. It features skateboarders and BMX and motocross riders who travel across the country, doing tricks to live music.

Tony has also made the leap from the world of skateboarding to the world of entertainment. He created a best-selling video game series, Tony Hawk's Pro Skater. He's starred in TV commercials and appeared on TV shows, including *Mad TV* and the *Simpsons*. He works for ESPN as a commentator for the X Games. He's also working on a movie about his life and an animated television show.

Tony also spends time with his family. He married his second wife, Erin, in 1996. They live in California with Riley and new sons Spencer and Keegan.

Tony with Erin, Spencer, and Keegan

Andy signs autographs for his fans

Andy is still skating professionally full-time. Whenever he skates, Andy always wears his signature yellow helmet and T-shirt. Andy spends much of his time working with skatepark designers. He travels to Europe and Asia to give skateboarding demonstrations. He can also be found at skateparks giving tips to his fans. When he's not on the road, Andy lives in San Diego with his wife, Rebecca.

One of Andy's proudest moments came when he starred in a Public Service Announcement (PSA) for the Partnership for a Drug-Free America. Andy doesn't smoke, drink, or do drugs, and he wants kids to know that they don't have to do those things to have fun as a pro skateboarder. His PSA was a big hit, and it led to Andy meeting President Bill Clinton in 1999. Andy even got to ride his board through the halls of the White House!

Andy meets President Clinton

And, of course, Tony and Andy can still be found skateboarding together. At the 2002 X Games in Philadelphia, the partners took home the gold again! Tony and Andy have been skateboarding together for so long, they almost make it look easy. Tony recently said, "We skate together so much that we can get in sync without even talking."

Tony Hawk and Andy Macdonald have helped transform skateboarding from a hobby to a pro sport. It wasn't easy for either rider to reach his goals and become the best. But after years of practice, hard work, and dedication, Tony and Andy were able to ride all the way to the top!

Andy and Tony—the dynamic duo!

Vocabulary

Air: riding your board with all four wheels off the ground

Bailing: pulling out of a trick early to avoid losing control of the board

Barge: skating in places where skateboarding is not allowed

Fakie: when a skater's board moves backward, but the skater remains facing forward

Flatland: a form of street skating in which tricks are performed on the pavement without other obstacles, such as stairs or curbs

Going Big: performing a trick either high in the air, over a large area or distance, or off a surface of extreme height

Goofy-footed: riding with the right foot in front of the board

Regular-footed: riding with the left foot on the front of the board

Slam: a fall that usually results in injury

Tweak: to move one's body during a trick

Wheelie: balancing on either the front two or back two wheels while riding

Anatomy of a Skateboard

Axle: a pin on which the wheel revolves

Bearings: small metal balls in the wheels that help them spin

Deck: the wood surface of a skateboard that riders stand on

Grip tape: a rough sandpaper sheet attached to the deck that helps the rider's feet stay gripped to the board

Nose: the front end of the skateboard

Rail: the outside edges of the skateboard and the plastic strips attached to the underside of the board

Tail: the back end of the skateboard

Trucks: the metal pieces on the front and back of the board that connect the wheels to the deck

Wheels: usually made of polyurethane. Different wheels are used for different kinds of riding